Poetry Book #18
by
Elliot M. Rubin

poetry book #18
by
Elliot M. Rubin

the photo on the cover
by Kristina Flour on Unsplash

Copyright Library of Congress
December 2020

ISBN - 978-1-7363641-0-9

No part of this book may be reproduced in any form whatsoever without the author's prior express written consent.
This book is fiction, and all names, people, places, and happenings are from the author's imagination and are used fictionally.
Any resemblance to any living or dead persons and/or businesses, locations, or events is coincidental in its entirety.
All rights reserved

Dedication
To my grandchildren
Shane, Isabelle, Jonathan, Carter,
Alexandra, Melanie, Mollie, and Madison

**In memory of my father
Herman S. Rubin
who wrote poetry all his life**

Special Thanks
to my *Zoom Critique Group*
for fine-tuning my poetry for this book:
Bill, Carol, David, Rodney, Sue, Rich, and Asha

Preface

I believe poetry is to be read and understood by all. It needs to be written in plain language for everyone's enjoyment.

Too often, poets write in-depth, penetrating poems where you need to be well-read and/or versed in literature's nuances to appreciate the poetry, not this book or any of my writings. I try to write so everyone can enjoy a few moments of intellectual satisfaction without consulting a dictionary or encyclopedia.

Table of Contents

baking 8
seasons 9
national loss 10
tears of Lady GaGa* 11
growing old 12
long division 13
death 14
masks 15
a car ride 16
stones 18
ivy 19
lamentation 20
rain 21
omens 22
at the market 23
breakup 24
waiting 25
memory loss 26
rubber band 27
tony's 1964 28
taboo 1961 29
say enough 30
night time 31
hips 32

high school kids 33

vanilla love 34

unknown 35

a poet's demise 36

my pals 37

time 38

someday 39

thirty days 40

3 am 41

mirrors 42

rapper 43

forbidden fruit 44

her secrets of love 45

the question 46

chaos 47

helpless 48

leaf 49

caring 50

denise 51

old summer love 52

turn off the news 53

the letter F poem 54

life bank account 55

solitary 56

writing 57
christmas memories 58

baking

the bakery hums in
early morning hours,
bread dough mixed,
panned, placed in ovens

a single girl works long hours
in the family business;
rarely dates, has a crush
on the flour-truck man

family cake recipes
secure in her mind,
never written down for
fear of being stolen

no one knows she keeps two
secrets; not even her parents
are aware there is more
than bread in her ovens

seasons

in spring, flowers bloom
their beauty pronounced,
so i pick one i like
to hold close to my heart

in summer, in the heat
of passion we are naked,
endless love never stops-
promises of forever

the fall brings cooler times
chill breezes temper us-
the flower starts to wilt;
death seems so imminent

winter temps freeze passion,
frosty winds from your mouth,
an icy heart stops our love;
waiting for it to end

in spring, flowers bloom
their beauty pronounced again,
i pick a new one this year
to hold close to my heart

national loss

i did not
know her,
only read
of her work

looks
didn't attract me,
only logic
did the trick

i grieve
at her passing-
the news
is kept off

somehow
she impressed me-
the future
now imperiled

a queen
of the court
stepped down
from her throne

the constitution
cries
for its lost
strong voice

goodbye
goodbye
notorious
RBG

tears of Lady GaGa*

tears of depression
roar down her cheek,
screaming,
 shrieking,
in quiet agony-
but no one hears

only her piano

melodies, tunes
do flow from her heart
telling the world
what her spirits
are now

writing the songs
speaks for **HER** self,
silence in public
curtains her feelings

thirty months withdrawn
from her other shadow,
finally, it lifts, then
she performs once again

*inspired by a 60 Minutes interview

growing old

i don't know
when it happened-
somehow
i evolved into my father,
grandfather,
even a few uncles-
television is off
except for news

i have aches, pains
never experienced before,
pills lined up
to the edge of the table

no more soda
    just water,
no more ketchup
    just salt,
no more running
    just walking

forget social meetings,
appointments are for doctors:
    feet,
    ears,
    eyes,
    heart,
    kidneys,
the list doesn't end

i need a parts store for people

long division

ten men
divided by
ten unsolved problems
equals one capable woman

death

it has been years
since we kissed
yet i still miss her;
she died in my heart
not in my arms-
she left me
for another love

masks

such a pretty face,
always smiling,
white teeth gleaming,
lush lips kissable,
waiting to be pressed

sometimes
looks are taken
at face value;
sometimes
it's a mask
to hide feelings
hidden
behind a façade

a car ride

i hate squeezing in the little car
with eleven other clowns
in full costume-
We are packed tighter
then the fat lady's vagina;
my nose is pushed into
Willie the Clown's bulbous rear
after he had franks and beans
for lunch- I have been practicing
breath control these last few shows

Sexy Suzy the Clown Bride
is behind me, sliding her arm
over my body, with her left hand
down my wide clown pants
as I try to push her arm off;
problem is she slides my hand away
onto Fireman Fred's crotch,
who thinks it is her!

I'm yelling at Mad Max the Clown,
our driver, to speed it up, but he yells
something back about fuel economy!
For Pete's sake, we only go fifty feet
into the center ring

Mad Max has a cattle prod which he zaps
my left foot with causing my body to gyrate
while Sexy Suzy is still amusing herself with me;
forcing my body to push against Willies back-
Out of costume, I now realize why he has that
silly smile when he sees me

After this show, I'm going to the ringmaster
to ask to work with the lion tamer-
I want to be the guy holding the gun with
live ammunition. When the clown car pulls up
I'm going to shoot them all,
except for Madge the Midget-
When I stand, she's the right height
to give me oral sex

she can live

stones

as i walk in life
there are stepping stones
to help me,
as there might be for others

with empathy in my heart
i can't bear
to overturn them,
for fear of what i might find

too much sorrow,
grief and hurt
for one person
to bear in a lifetime

how can i help them
when their agony
so overcomes my
heart- i cry out

at the inhumanity
others suffer; with
little solace or
care afforded them

where is God?

ivy

the ivy grew
taking years to wrap
itself around the massive,
tall peach tree until it enveloped
all its branches, suffocating
the life force from it,
its growth stopped

after many years
he did the same thing
to her,
until the ivy was dying,
after the tree which sustained it
was no longer viable

a forest ranger cut the vine off-
replanted a branch
far from the deadly ivy
saving its future

the tree once again grew,
its life saved by a girlfriend
who only showered love on her,
allowing the leaves to sprout

once again

lamentation

although i admire its looks
the beautiful rose is alone
amongst others, yet i cannot
touch it or even hold it

the thorns of society
prevent approaching,
only the lightest whisp
of conversation permitted

the reddest rose among roses
i am drawn to it like bees
to pollen, only to be stung
and denied imagined happiness

my vine is entangled with another
thicket preventing me from leaving,
my roots are now too deep in the soil;
i can only admire from afar

rain

no, i will not complain
about the rain today,
gloomy weather fits

water feeds the roots
nourishing the world,
how can i protest

my tears cannot compare
with a heartbreak event
when i read of so many dead

a pandemic abatement denied
due to narcissistic incompetence,
with everyday people believing

the sheep march on to the slaughter

omens

when:
our ring bearer pawned the ring,
the church burned down the day before,
our parents forgot the exact day, never showed up,
the airline went on strike, canceling our honeymoon,
our baker sent a cheery, happy birthday cake,
the florist sent three condolence wreaths,
and the priest married two groomsmen, not us

i thought it an omen on my marriage to be

so we just shacked up for fifty years-
why tempt fate?

at the market

i watch in awe
as the butcher,
with massive forearms
lifts the cleaver,
brings it down
through flesh,
sinew,
bone-
passionless,
dicing and slicing
discarding renderings to the trash

reminds me of you
in so many ways;
except you smiled
when you left;
my heart tattered,
broken in pieces
to move on to your
next lover

what page
am i
in your thick,
never-ending diary?

breakup

the feathers
on the floor
told me
what to expect;
the demon from within
slid out
from her netherworld
to confront my heart,
destroying our love,
stomping on her
angels wings
to end our romance

forever

waiting

everyone is waiting
for something

our special person
our car to be fixed
our child to start to walk
our winning lottery ticket

one event we all
have in common:
we wait for death

what's important
though,
is what we do
while we wait

memory loss

i remember her sometimes-
a scent that lingers
in a person's mind
for decades, tumbling
into consciousness,
stirring memories
forgotten

when i go shopping
the perfume counter
awakens thoughts
of a past love
long gone years ago-
oh, how i miss her

my nurse wears it too-
she takes care of me
every day, all my needs;
funny thing, i notice

we wear matching wedding bands

rubber band

as i sit at my desk
the rubber band is
next to my pen, waiting
to wrap around something

it reminds me of
the unseen band that kept
my girl and i together
for these so many years

unfortunately, she
thought the elasticity
meant she could date others
then bounce back to love me

with time the band changes,
gets brittle, no longer
elastic, useless, and
is discarded, like her

tony's 1964

tony's drive-in burger place
is no more-
the teenage waitresses
grew up and married,
the carhop service
is gone too-
a fast-food chain
replaced it

only memories are left

brought back
with every burger
and greasy fries
my tongue tastes
from a roadside
new jersey diner;
brought to me by
an aged, divorced,
haggard waitress
as i try to recapture
a long past 1964
epicurean delight

taboo 1961

i never saw a black rose
up close before,
my eyes were bolted
on its beauty,
the fluidity,
the shape,
the softness of its petals;
yet i was prevented
from holding it
other than momentarily

there were only white roses
in my past,
no other colors-

how could i even think
   of taking it home?
how do i explain it
   to my parents?
how do i tell them
   i want to keep it?

forever

no, i couldn't-
i held a white rose
in my grasp,
never letting it go

today is a different era-
i am now free to say
without hesitation,
black roses are beautiful

say enough

they were together
a long time,
building a home
for themselves
with their kids
until she died
after twelve years

it was a good union,
typical in many ways

vacations, family,
fun times and sorrow,
late-night conversations,
yet he has regrets-
maybe he didn't
tell her more times
how much he loved,
cherished her,
say what his heart felt

now it's too late

he didn't say enough

night time

the house is quiet

i sit alone in silence
with a ripe honeydew
on my table

my knife cuts small
cubes then place them
on a plate until there
is nothing left to slice

slowly, i savor each piece
as the sweetness brings back
a rush of good memories
we had together

i miss you terribly

since your death
evenings are so lonely

hips

everyone has hips;
men,
women,
lovers,

everyone enjoys hips,
watching them
coming or going

lovers caress hips
once they touch their hearts,
they also break hearts
as they walk away

high school kids

he sat in the bleachers
watching cheerleaders
jumping around, prancing
on the field below

one stood out with
long, dark brown hair,
short skirt, and a face
he longed to kiss but couldn't

the chess club, debating team
and honor society is where
he hung out in high school;
sports guys all wanted her

she was part of the in-crowd,
he wasn't. one day, her group
sat at his lunch table talking
about something from class

they didn't understand a topic
so he spoke up and explained it-
after a lengthy discussion
she thanked him, then left

they ran into each other in the hall;
she again thanked him, then
walked to class together
as she grabbed his hand in hers

decades later, they still hold hands

vanilla love

nothing unusual
going on here,
just the vanilla
type of love
one settles into
after many years
of being together

no longer enjoying
a peppermint tryst
to spice it up,
or cherry syrup
splayed across
to sweeten it a bit

forget the neopolitan tri flavor,
no, not even sometimes

once, i even tried
 to bring in another flavor-
   european chocolate was too intense
     for my taste,
      i overdosed,
        i liked it
          too much

i'm back to vanilla

unknown

at ten,
she sharpens her design skills
as she completes her look
with the addition of a red sash
draped over a green party dress
from shoulder to hip,
adding sparkling toy rings
on her fingers

at eighty-two sitting alone,
dressed in an ivory ball gown
with plastic pearl earrings and
a crystal necklace around her neck
in her one-room apartment,
the food on her plate
barely touched, the hot tea cold,
she leans her head
against yellowed wallpaper
then closes her eyes

she starts to dream
of her youth
with a future
never attained

a poet's demise

his pad and pen
are next to his bed,
beside the telephone
and television remote-
he keeps it there
so he can write prompts
when a thought flashes
in his mind

family, agent, and publisher are there,
waiting for the final breath of death-
beloved for years
his poetry read all over the world

he hears a long, loud,
never-ending beep-
people crying,
the nurse tells everyone
hearing is the last to go-
his eyes go dark,
his mind still going

i guess this is it,
a new adventure;
if only i could jot
a few notes down;
my pad is only
by my shoulder.
why can't i move my arms,
why can't....

my pals

gone,
they are almost all gone-
we were eight guys
on the same street

we played ball together,
hung around,
chased girls,
double-dated

as i age
aches and pains
are constant constraints-
no more running around

to be honest,
today
i have more doctors
than friends

time

just a little more time

holding your hand in mine
as we walk together,
the first kiss was so sweet
it felt like heaven on earth,
our embrace as lovers
is ecstasy to me;
i didn't want it to stop-
each moment went so quick,
our lives went so fast

time…

i want just a little more

someday

someday
the ride will be over,
the merry-go- round
will stop-
i'll be out of tickets,
no more music
or laughing
with family and friends

i've been luckier
than a lot of others,
people i've known
and loved
have left the ride
before me,
sometimes in their youth
or middle age

i held a lot of tickets
in my hands when the ride started,
but somehow
the conductor
seemed to take them so quickly,
 i never noticed them gone
until the ride started
to slow down-
i realized
it's time
to get

off

thirty days

we dated for thirty days;
she wanted it in many ways
just another dating craze;
to me, it was a foggy haze

she had a thing for thirty days
then we just parted ways
dating her was like a maze
every time i'm in a daze

i had to stop before i died
she loved me, she only lied-
tears aplenty she cried and cried,
i'm exhausted, i almost died

3 am

it's three in the morning-
my mind starts to churn,
creative thoughts bubble up
forcing me to write them down

"not another morning of writing?"
she asks as i put on slippers,
not understanding
creativity
is as fleeting as life itself

mirrors

a mirror is a fantastic thing,
it reflects what we put in front
if we feel pretty, that's what we see,
and the reverse is also true too

i never look in a mirror,
to affect my feelings
and start my day
your face is all i need,

rapper

i saw her talk
   in rhythm
toss her head
   side to side
smoke a blunt
spit out words
hand signs
   only the hood knows
shoot to fame
cash too much
cars too many
bloodsuckers
   left and right
nite life never ends

then life changed

lil sis od'd one nite
   almost joined michael and prince

mom distraught
   a broken heart
   took her to heaven

a wake-up cry

it called sis
   back to before,
no more drugs
no more nites

rapped a new tune

forbidden fruit

at a friend's pool party
in the garden of eden
sitting poolside
with my feet in the water,
when eve sat beside me
wearing a small knit
bikini with her apples
ripe and bountiful;
as she placed her hand
on my inner thigh
offering me forbidden fruit
from her curvaceous tree

then she stood,
her curvy roots staring in my face,
a soft voice whispering, *"we can talk later"*

sensing my angel of death
somewhere close, i smiled,
declined to take a bite of her fruit

she walked away

"you should have taken up her offer,"
the snake next to me said
as he slithered after eve

her secrets of love

past
lovers,
current ones,
placed in her safe,
she knows
the combination

secrets known
to those who've been
gifted her essence,
tasted the sweetness
of her vault
can speak of it

husbands come and go,
fly along like the wind,
experienced and forgotten
waiting for her next love

the door to her safe
locked tight,
the combination
in her mind,
rarely revealed to anyone,
accessible only
through her heart

the question

it happens way too much-
in the beginning,
hands held,
kisses linger,
warmth cloaks the soul

eventually
a question pops up,
things cool down,
kisses don't linger

hands get cold,
hearts harden-
is love an emotion
or an obligation?

chaos

the mud in the universe
falls on us all the time-
things get gooey,
life is not smooth,
plans go awry
for no logical reason,
something tells me
this is wrong,
yet tomorrow
seems to be here
before i realize it

things do get done,
plans do get finalized,
the good and the bad
seem to coexist in the end

somehow

i stand tall,
i am okay,
i don't worry anymore;

i now realize chaos happens

i'll be okay

helpless

i loved her many years ago-
late one evening
the angel of death visited

she took her own life;
in her mind,
only she knew why

the bathtub filled,
stretched out,
a new razor,
swift, deep slice,
a life force
oozed out

her body slid
inch by inch
below burgundy stained water,
long brown hair
floated

young, seventeen, bright, cheerful
nobody suspected

we were dating;
intense, in love.
no fights or arguments

years later
i met and married-
my daughter
is named after her

true love never dies

leaf

i seldom notice the green leaves
fluttering on the trees outside,
they are just there

walking along in early autumn,
a large leaf blocked my path,
stunning dark crimson and
medium ochre
i stopped to stare
at its beauty in death

leaves know change
is in the air,
they know summer
will be over
leaving its comfort
and nourishment,
beginning a
death knell with
stunning colors,
as frost approaches

too bad people
don't recognize
autumnal changes
in relationships
until too late;
until one walks out
breaking a heart,
their love died a long time
before winter comes along

caring

where is the caring,
the humility, the warmth,
help for people
in need of assistance

how do we melt iron hearts,
build smiles with hugs
discarding cold shoulders,
put the human back in humanity?

denise

her mannerisms theatrical,
hands trapezing in the air,
elongated pronunciation
mimicking a british accent,
trying to impress
when first we met

she forgot we went to school in Brooklyn-
guys wrote her name in the boy's room
in high school;
that was forty years ago

we connected at a widow social,
her beauty maintained,
she attracted men
yet no one stuck around
after a quick conversation

i felt compassion,
she overcompensated,
trying to be desirable, i thought-
afterward, i asked to have
coffee down the street

sitting in a diner late at night,
a quiet place, she calmed down;
her accent gone,
we spoke as lonely adults
trying to find a path forward in life

we exchanged numbers-
i didn't call, i waited
for her to take the first step-
a year later, she moved in

old summer love

for the winter
my summer clothes
are put away
until spring
arrives again

we had a great time
laughing and loving
last summer
when we first met

in the fall
we went home
calling and writing,
can't wait till summer
to see you again

but your response
was not expected-
seems your feelings
are like my clothes,
in storage for the winter

turn off the news

why do children die like that?
deaths happen all the time,
all year round,
never stops-
every kind of illness;
some so gruesome
they qualify as torture,
yet deaths continue

unabated

all the reasons are known
all the cures are tried
all the prayers are said

is there a god?

the letter F poem

Fred fancies Francis
    fornicates,
Faith feels forsaken

Lune (known as American Haiku)
5 3 5 syllables

life bank account

everyone
has a bank account-
the problem is
no one knows
the exact balance

placed in it

every day we live
a withdrawal is made
reducing the balance

deposits are not allowed
or even considered;
yet sometimes
a major withdrawal
is postponed,
a loan made by medical science
keeps the principal intact

still, we don't know
what's left in it

solitary

alone in my mind

    silence rings aloud,

        darkness envelops,

            legs twitch uncontrolled,

        images appear

      flashes of my past,

    hours never end, days merge,

the meds will
            wear
              off

soon the nurse will let me out

if she remembers

writing

great writers
sometimes
experience events
on the edge of danger,
risking life and limb
so they can write of it

poets must live
a voracious life
observing then,
committing everything
to memory-
writing
not from their mind
but from their heart,
so their words
can reach yours

christmas memories

remember looking out the window
hoping for snow to start,
bare tree limbs, arms outstretched,
waiting to catch virgin white snow

mom hanging empty stockings,
with last years garland hung,
wishing tomorrow morning
your name is on a present or two

trying hard to remember
if you were good all year,
pretty sure you did okay,
yet doubt lingers for awhile

cookies and milk left out
in case santa wants a snack,
maybe to make amends,
in case you slipped up

waking early the next morning
you jump out of bed
to look under the tree,
where your gifts were to be

those christmas mornings
live on in memories-
they visit every year,
haunting

they never change

Other books of poetry by Elliot M. Rubin

Scrambled Poems from my Heart
A Boutique Bouquet of Poems and Stories
Rumblings of an Old Man
Surf Avenue Girl - semi episodic poems
Flash Pan Poetry
Unrequited Love
Aliyah - an Episodic Memoir
My Life if I Took a Different Path -
   an Episodic Memoire
Bent Twigs and Wet Feet
Stories of the South - semi episodic poems
Selected Poems by Elliot M. Rubin
Chains of Love and other Poems
Cookies and milk with poetry
Paper + pen = poetry
Love Balcony and other poems
Enjoyable Humanist Poetry
Poetry Book #17

www.CreativeFiction.net

follow me on Instagram at
Elliot_M_Rubin
humanist poetry